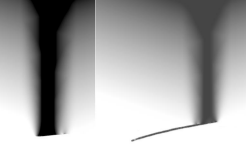

GOSPEL REFLECTIONS

FOR SUNDAYS OF YEAR A: MATTHEW

ISBN 978 1 910248 32 4

Designed by Messenger Publications Design Department
Printed in Ireland by Turners

MESSENGER
PUBLICATIONS
JESUITS in IRELAND

Messenger Publications,
37 Lower Leeson Street, Dublin 2
www.messenger.ie

GOSPEL
REFLECTIONS
FOR SUNDAYS OF YEAR A: MATTHEW

DONAL NEARY SJ

The author is grateful to Logos Press, in whose missalette these reflections were originally published (Logos Missalette, Greystones, Co. Wicklow).

CONTENTS

HOLY DAYS

Other books by the author include,
More Masses with Young People (The Columba Press)
Who Do You Say That I am? (Veritas)
Gospel Reflections for Sundays of Year C: Luke
(Messenger Publications),
and many books of prayer for the seasons of the church year.

He frequently writes for *The Sacred Heart Messenger,*
of which he is editor.

INTRODUCTION

In these reflections, I have tried to find a connecting thread between the gospel story, faith and ordinary life. It expands on consistent themes of St Ignatius of Loyola, 'finding God in all things', or 'searching for God in all things'.

What the book is *not*, is an exegesis or scriptural commentary on the gospel, or a link between all the readings. Many books highlight these areas. The reflections also help towards the preparation of a theme for Sundays in a liturgy group, or as preparation for hearing the gospel reading or reflecting on it during the week.

The book aims to refresh our insight into well-known scripture. Mostly we know the gospel readings each Sunday very well – some we have heard many times. Scripture is always old, and always new. We help each other to see new aspects to a story. This can be in a sharing group or through reading books on the gospels. I hope that this book will give a new light into the scripture, as I always like when someone says, or when I say myself, 'That's a new way of looking on that story; I never saw it like that before'. *Gospel Reflections for Sundays of Year A* brings the searchings of our heart to the word of the gospel and to finding God bit by bit in our lives.

In this method we may recognise what Pope Francis said on finding God: 'Our life is not given to us like an opera libretto, in which all is written down; but it means going, walking, doing, searching, seeing ... We must enter into the adventure of the quest for meeting God; we must let God search and encounter us' (Interview with Antonio Spadaro SJ, November 2013).

Above all, may they bring us closer to the Lord Jesus who wants to come close to us in his word, and his word is a human, loving word, rooted in our lives and in his preaching and mission.

Donal Neary SJ

1ST SUNDAY OF ADVENT

Light for the journey

In faith and in hope we begin Advent this week with its first candle. With Mary and Joseph we wait for Christ. The candles are lighting the way for them – and for us! The coming light of Jesus lights both our waiting and our journey in life. May it shine the light of Christ into the darknesses of the year since last Christmas – bereavement, illness, depression, disappointments?

We prepare best for Christmas by spreading this light. The way to celebrate Christmas is rooted in our following of the gospel. Among our ways are care for the poor, some daily prayer, and the wish to forgive and be forgiven.

All the different images of Christmas prepare us for this birth – the carols we hear and sing, the lights in the streets, the star over the church and the ways we pray with anticipation and remember other Christmas days with joy.

Everything of this month can remind us of God. The Christmas trees, lights, cards, carols, parties, Santa hats, the houses lit up with reindeer and all the things we see about Christmas, all remind us that God is near.

We welcome this light in the spirit of Pope Francis: 'Those who have opened their hearts to God's love, heard his voice and received his light, cannot keep this gift to themselves. Since faith is hearing and seeing, it is also handed on as word and light' (*The Light of Faith*, 37).

Remember some people or memories that make you grateful for Christmas. Thank God for these in your own world.
Come, Lord Jesus. Come into our world of gold and grey, into the world, which needs you badly.

2ND SUNDAY OF ADVENT

The straight way

Before the motorways a journey took ages, with twists and turns, corners and hills. Now much has been made straight.

John's message was that we would live along a path where words and actions match, and where kindness matches convictions.

John the Baptist was a man on one mission – to be the messenger of the one he did not know. His life had a vision and a purpose, like when we are really committed to people or to causes or to the poor or to peace in the world. John was the man of desert food and desert dress; he took time out to find what the biggest thing in life was and then kept following it, often not knowing where it would go.

The human heart is complicated and we know that. We need that one who will touch our hearts with love and forgiveness and guide us himself in ways that are straight, and whose hand will guide us along straight paths when we need it.

God's guiding is gentle. John found that Jesus was a gentler guide: no name-calling, no bringing the axe to the tree, but calling each of us his friend, and nourishing the tree rather than cutting it down.

Jesus would melt the snow to make a path, not hack at it and destroy in the process. Our hearts can be melted by the love of God and love of others.

Think of or remember a time when you made a decision
to follow the way of Jesus. Offer this to him again.
Lord God, make our hearts like yours.

3RD SUNDAY OF ADVENT

Good news of God

John the Baptist was a man of passionate commitment to what he believed in. He strongly believed in the coming of the Christ. This man of faith was being tested in that Jesus was a different type of Christ or Messiah from what he expected. He often wondered who the Messiah would be.

John was a man with a lot of conviction and truth. He preached what he believed. He practised what he taught.

But he seemed to miss the point sometimes. He seemed to miss that Jesus would be found, not in preaching only but in helping others. John preached repentance for sin; Jesus preached the coming of the kingdom.

The blind would see, and the lame would walk – these were to be signs of the coming of the 'One to come'.

Pope Francis says: 'There is no prayer in which Jesus does not inspire us to do something.' Our faith in Jesus is seen in strong action. The poor are helped at our pre-Christmas collections. We might ask not what we might get for Christmas, but how our Christmas might help others. We might ask that Christmas will be happy for others because of us – happy in body, with enough food for every family, happy in mind that we know the truth of God's coming into the world, and happy in forgiveness, as that is one of God's biggest gifts.

What is the good news of Jesus for you just now?
Lord, let me believe that your life is good news and share this good news with all I meet in word and action.

4ᵀᴴ SUNDAY OF ADVENT

Call to Joseph

In religious terms we would call Joseph a faithful type of guy, observant in religious thought and practice. The visit from the angel tests his faithfulness to God and to Mary. He doesn't let them down. He was called to be the carer of Jesus and Mary and to find a new openness to the mystery of God.

A temptation of religion is to tie things down too much. The law in Joseph's time was strict – if a woman was pregnant the man would cancel the betrothal, and she might be stoned to death! Joseph went beyond law to love and the mystery of God's call. Good religion is open to the mystery of life, however life challenges us and calls us.

Some of the most open-minded people I have met have been very religious, and some of the most narrow-minded people have also been religious! Like good and bad medicine, there is good and bad in religion.

True religion is open to mystery. We need a church lit with the light of God, as Joseph was. His burden was lifted when he was open to God, to take Mary home as his wife, no matter what others might think.

This is the annunciation to Joseph – the word of God from the angel to Joseph in a dream. It opened him to a huge new meaning in life. We accept this word as a central part of our lives, and the next time we meet the word, it will be made flesh.

Picture your house, and all who live in it.
Imagine the light of Christ in each room and on all.
Lord, you are the word of God, who is made flesh, have mercy on us.

CHRISTMAS DAY

Welcome to God and from God

Most homes have a crib of some sort; it is part of our Christmas. It brings the mystery of the birth of Jesus into our homes. Some church cribs have an open front – a sign that all are welcome. Many people feel unwelcome in the church – people in second and other relationships that cause questions, people who have been through crime or in prison, people in addiction, families who feel the worse for what some family members have done, people of homosexual orientation, former priests and religious. Like the shepherds at the first crib, all are welcome. The church welcomes all at this time of the year and, indeed, always. May we welcome all as God does, with the compassion and love of God?

Christmas reminds us to deal with each other in love and compassion. Someone was very harsh on someone when speaking to me recently. I just said, 'God loves him, and I would prefer to be with God on this one'. Just as we take a while to know the full story of Jesus, we take a while to know the full story of everyone.

We pray at the Mass that we may come to share the divinity of Christ who comes to share in our humanity.

> *Remember those you wish to pray for at Christmas;*
> *pray with your breathing – with every outbreath*
> *simply say a name you wish to remember in prayer.*
> *And maybe pray this Sufi prayer:*
> *Your Light is in all forms, Your Love in all beings.*
> *Allow us to recognise You/in all your holy names and forms.*

FEAST OF THE HOLY FAMILY

Celebrating family life

We often remember the sacrifices our parents made for us. Financial generosity, giving their time, understanding us when we go wrong. The first family story of Jesus is a tough story – Joseph caring for him and Mary through the dangers of the journey into Egypt and back, like asylum seekers or refugees today fleeing from danger in their country.

We salute the love of parents, siblings, guardians, grandparents and extended families; we remember at different times of life how much they did for us and gave to us.

In the difficulties of family life today, the role of the church is to support family life of all kinds – with education, faith-formation, supporting political structures that support family life, being there for families in bad times like illness and death, and providing a place to celebrate family life in marriage and baptism. Parishes try to be committed to supporting family life.

Jesus came not only to be with us, but to care. This is the call to the church – being in the world and being for the world.

'Joseph took the child and his mother.' He was a caring man, looking after them, making a huge difference to a small number of people – this is the message of love in the gospel and is the central message of the feast today.

Remember in prayer those in your family for whom you are grateful.
As you picture each person, say thanks to the Lord for him or her.
Lord, care for our families and may we in our families
care for each other.

2ND SUNDAY AFTER CHRISTMAS

Glory and joy

Would you expect to find glory in the crib? It is there in human and the divine love. Angels sing of glory to God ... this is the biggest thing that ever happened the world. God among us, the word made flesh! Love has come among us like never before.

As the gospel of John goes on there is another sense of that glory. Glory means not just angels and bright light – it is the love of God and then our love.

Jesus comes with the love of God. He makes a difference, calling us to be a community of people who find, through their faith and humanity, the motivation to care for each other always, in good times and bad.

That's all part of the message of Christmas. God our creator passionately wants a world where people are cherished and human rights are respected, within a way of life where the rights of all, especially the poor, are met. This child is for the world, and his life and ministry will bring compassion to us and danger to him.

Christmas is about Jesus being for us, about the church being for the world of today. It is an annual reminder that our call is to allow Jesus into our hearts in love, and to allow him out in our love of those near to us, and of the wider world.

Imagine the Christmas scene, and notice that behind the manger
there is a cross. This is the child who will save us.
With the angels and the shepherds, with Mary and Joseph,
we welcome you, Lord Jesus.

BAPTISM OF THE LORD

You are beloved

Jesus' baptism by John the Baptist had a different meaning from ours. It was more a baptism of sorrow for sin, and of forgiveness; in this plunge into the river, Jesus identified with his people in his baptism.

At the baptism he heard the best words he could hear: You are my beloved. God led Jesus to John to hear these words.

One of us, one with us, he could now be one for us. Joy flooded his heart as he heard these words. Something happened for Jesus at that moment that only he could know – like bells ringing that only he could hear. Have you heard it in your life? At times we face the huge mysteries of love, beauty, friendship, birth, death. And we know, in the middle of it all, that we are beloved.

Our call is to be involved fully in life and love. The Christian is called to be with others at the times of need, of depth and mystery. Jesus did that – plunging himself into our humanity and with all of us.

The feast of the baptism is of something new for all. The son of God is one of us. We have a new way of knowing God not just in the laws of old but in the new Spirit of Jesus.

So let the bells of love ring for us in God; and wherever we find it; let's ring bells of love for all the most needy of God's people.

Let the word 'beloved' echo in your mind and heart.
This is God's word to you today.
Lord, thanks for calling me beloved.

IST SUNDAY IN LENT

Co-creators

Jesus is tempted to use creation just for himself.

This can happen with money, other people, the environment and religion. We are called to look after God's creation, not control it.

To be co-workers with God is our call – to focus on people as well as plans, to feel the needs here and abroad.

One view of God is that he looks after the world for good or bad, and we are just the receivers. The other is that we are co-workers in developing the world and God's creation. Jesus was tempted to throw himself away from the world as he knew it, but he did not. He would live by the word of God, and God would care for him as for the parents in the first reading.

'A Christian who doesn't safeguard creation, who doesn't make it flourish, is a Christian who isn't concerned with God's work, that work born of God's love for us' (Pope Francis, 2015).

The temptation to Jesus was to take him off the path of his father. Like him, we are often tempted to use the creation of God just for our benefit. Our call is to be co-creators of the world with God.

Imagine a garden where everything is beautiful. It is the 'creation'
of a gardener. Then imagine that someone has ruined one corner of it
– notice the difference. Apply this to how we treat God's creation.
May we care for your creation, O Lord, with the love
you have for creation and for us.

2ND SUNDAY IN LENT

On the mountain

The hours on the mountain were a huge experience for Peter, James and John, who would always be with him. They saw him in his glory, the beloved son of the Father. There was more to him than meets the eye.

You climb a mountain and you see new views, you see the city from a new vantage point. You see the countryside in its beauty. We need times to climb mountains and get away from the ordinary. Lent is a time like that – as we give something up, we take something on.

From the mountain, we now return home with a good seed: the seed of the Word of God. The Lord will send rain and that seed will grow. It will grow and it will bear fruit. We thank the Lord for the seed but we also want to thank the sower because you were the sower and you know how to do it.' (Pope Francis, 2014)

Whenever we climb the mountain of the Lord or make any journey with him, we are changed. As every mountain is different, so every moment with him is well worth while!

We receive this word of God and we receive our call to share it. The apostles would spend their lives sharing what they got on the mountain, and how it changed them.

Is there a word or line of scripture that you like and which helps you?
Repeat it to yourself as a prayer.
Lord, make me a listener to your word.

3RD SUNDAY IN LENT

The well is deep

A famous picture has the Samaritan woman looking into the well and seeing there her image – and the image of Jesus. In the depths of the well of her life is the presence of Jesus.

In the depths of the well, when we are in love, pain, death, decision, joy, we find God. God is near when we are near to ourselves, even in shame and sin. We thirst for meaning in life, for knowing we are totally loved, for community and companionship – and God offers all this.

This is the offering of God – the living water is the Holy Spirit. We thirst for inclusion – the disciples in this story did not want Jesus talking to a woman. So much of the religion of the time separated people. In the depths of the well we are all equal.

We find the mercy of God in the well. As we go into the depths of prayer and ourselves we are open to mercy. We may put conditions on God's mercy – naming our sins, or numbering them. At the bottom of the well is the water of mercy.

Of the mercy of God, Pope Francis says that 'there is no sin or crime of any kind that can erase from the mind or heart of God even one of the children he has created' (November 2013).

Imagine yourself looking into a well; see the face of Jesus looking at you from its depths. He looks at you with love.
Lord, send me the living water of the Holy Spirit.

4ᵀᴴ SUNDAY IN LENT

The eye of faith

Some saw a blind man being cured and walked on amazed. Others saw the same cures and found faith. We can see things – everyday things – with different eyes. A sick woman may be seen with the eye of compassion for illness, hope for a cure, profit for a profession. The Christian tries to see the world with the eye of faith.

Faith grows in many ways – by opening ourselves to our human desire for God, by mulling over the good things of life, by experiencing the good within ourselves, by looking over times of faith in the past and by allowing the goodness of others to bring us to new and stronger faith. This is the call of the gospel today – to open our eyes to the Lord who is at work in many ways.

We learn to see and love with the eye of faith by looking at the look of Jesus towards us. It is often a big jump to believe in what we cannot see. Even the blind man today was reminded that 'you are looking at the Son of Man, he is speaking to you'. Jesus looks at each of us with faith in our goodness and with love.

Maybe we can walk around in this atmosphere of faith, 'seeing' God in a flower, in a parent holding a child's hand, in a person pushing a wheelchair with courage, and notice that in many ways God is near and the presence of Jesus is at hand.

Let this verse echo in your mind: Amazing Grace – I once was lost
and now am found, was blind and now I see.
Lord, let me see you in the simple things of my life.

11:1–45

5ᵀᴴ SUNDAY IN LENT

A human heart

When people read this they say they see that Jesus is a real human being, son of God, God of heaven, man of the earth, weeping over a friend.

His was a human heart. He liked friends and he found a home and a safe place with them, over the hill and away from the mob. We might picture him there – the talk, the chat, the prayers, the love; meals with other friends who dropped in, times of prayer and silence.

The one who can share a laugh, eat a scone, have a drink or a cuppa. The one who'd give a wink at the sign of peace! Not always so serious, even about religion. There's no such thing as a sad saint!

He is a good friend. Friendship gives new spirit.

When life is ending we will give thanks for friends, and regret the way we have drifted or hurt each other. Real friendship is when another's thoughts and life become at least as or more important than our own.

So the resurrection and the life is not just for after death. It is for now. We raise each other up in friendship and in love. In that is the grace of the Lord, himself a friend, for when we love, God lives in us.

Picture your friends and those you love and
give thanks to God for each of them.
Lord, help me to keep love and friendship alive in my life.

PALM SUNDAY

He has endured the cross

Our gospel today is long; it is the first of two readings of the passion and death of Jesus; we hear many sayings and notice events that are familiar to us and to all Christians. Maybe during the week we could take time to reread the gospel account, and watch what happens, going a bit behind the externals.

We will see Jesus being mocked, tortured, hurt, ridiculed, beaten and killed. We notice his fear in the garden of his agony, and also his willingness to go to the end for what he believes in and sees as his mission in life. We see him being treated unjustly, and a notorious thief being chosen over him for release. We see him on the cross, when he seems to feel neglected by his Father.

We notice also the help he received – the silent sympathy and love of his mother, Simon's help carrying the cross, the sympathy of the 'daughters of Jerusalem', and even the faith of the Roman who said he was a good man, a 'son of God'. We wonder about how he felt with the mockery and with the help he received.

We can identify with much of his suffering, in our own lives and the lives of people close to us. He is the one who 'has endured the cross and despised its shame' (Hebrews).

We can often take comfort and consolation from the fact that he identifies with the suffering of the human race, and that his resurrection is the basis of our faith, hope and love.

Look at or imagine a crucifix, and pray as you feel drawn.
Lord, by your cross and resurrection, you have set us free;
you are the Saviour of the world.

EASTER SUNDAY

Alleluia – for singing, not for humming!

The reason for the joy of Easter is that Christ is risen – the women who came to the tomb found their joy in this. They may have found joy also in a beautiful dawn in the garden, or in their friendships, but the joy of Easter is a joy of faith, which nothing need take away.

The joy of the resurrection is a joy in giving the life we have received from God: 'Life grows by being given away, and it weakens in isolation and comfort. Indeed, those who enjoy life most are those who leave security on the shore and become excited by the mission of communicating life to others' (Pope Francis). The Alleluia is for singing, not for humming; it is to be heard from the voice of the heart, and should lift the hearts of those who hear: 'Jesus Christ is risen. He is risen indeed. Alleluia!'

We often see great joy in the middle of huge poverty: often the poor can live for the present moment and enjoy it to the full. Sometimes in the middle of illness we find a peace we don't know from where it comes. The grace of the risen Jesus can touch our lives at any time. Let's not be like Christians 'whose lives seem like Lent without Easter' (Pope Francis). Having lived through the joyful season of Lent, our hearts are wholly lifted now in joy received and joy given.

> *Breathe in and out: on the inbreath echo the word 'joy';*
> *on the outbreath echo the word 'thanks'.*
> *Risen Christ, raise our lives in joy.*

2ND SUNDAY OF EASTER

Thanks, Thomas!

Thomas ... thanks! For bringing honesty into our faith. He didn't pretend that he was better than he was. He began by wanting proof and ended by being glad of faith. He is the patron saint of transitions and steps in faith. Faith is a journey. He is the saint of faith in our times. The community was the place he found faith, having lost it when he tried to go it alone. Then he came back to the community of faith and went on a journey of life that took him to martyrdom in India.

He also found Christ in wanting to touch his wounds. We find God when we enter into his wounds in the wounds of our world.

In the faith community of the church we can keep our faith. Our faith grows here too. Thomas looked for faith by wanting to touch the wounds of Jesus. When Jesus invited him to do so, he found he didn't need to. He found faith in being present with the wounded Christ and discovered there his faith in the glory of Christ.

We can do the same. What was said to Thomas is said to us all: 'You believe because you can see me. Blessed are those who have not seen and yet believe.'

Recall those who have strengthened your faith and be grateful;
picture each person and pray for each of them.
Lord, I believe, strengthen my belief.

3ᴿᴰ SUNDAY OF EASTER

Hearts uplifted

I have met many people who found this story really helped at times when they were down, when there were disappointments in life, when they encountered illness and many of the crosses of life. They believed in him after he had vanished, having broken bread with them. He had accompanied them in a dark journey of life.

Jesus went to them – he did not await their visit. Somehow he knew that people of his 'set' were in darkness and maybe despair. This is the call of the church – to be with us in prayer, community and service always, and especially for what Pope Francis calls 'the peripheries of life'. Most of us spend some time there, and appreciate the help of love and faith.

Then they went to tell the story of how they were changed. Faith grows through sharing it. A father said, 'At my child's first communion, my faith became stronger'.

They told their story of Jesus in the here and now, sometimes reminiscing on what things were once like in Galilee. Every journey of life can be an Emmaus journey where we meet the Lord. Every altar can be the altar of Emmaus, and indeed every meal can be a time of friendship, care and nourishment for body and for soul.

*Notice this week where the Lord is present in love, care, creation,
an uplift of joy, prayer and the Eucharist.
Lord, lift my hope and my faith in your presence as the disciples
found their hearts burning when they listened to you.*

4ᵀᴴ SUNDAY OF EASTER: VOCATIONS SUNDAY

Follow in Love

The first big moment of vocation is baptism. The anointing of chrism at baptism might be called the anointing for vocation.

The baptismal vocation is for witness, love and service. This is expressed in ways in which people live out their baptism in married life, single life – and within the single life, maybe religious life or priesthood.

Our active witness is to the life and the values of Jesus in our lives. Teaching is not itself a vocation, for example, but the way we teach is a way of living out our vocation. It is the same with many of the helping professions and employments. Being a good neighbour can be a living out of our vocation.

We witness to love in marriage, in family, extended family, and in friendship. Any love is a sharing in the love of God. In the moments of unselfish love in any relationship we are living out our vocation. When we love, we are doing God's will!

We witness to service in the wider world in our care for the poor and in welcoming the stranger.

In a place of silence, let the words 'Come, follow me'
echo in your mind and heart.
Lord, be with me as I offer myself in partnership with you
to work in your world.

5TH SUNDAY OF EASTER

The centre holds

The gospel presents Jesus as the guide in life, the 'way, truth and life'. The Christian centre is the person of Christ. Our work for Jesus and our love for people, no matter what our calling in life, flow from this. Mother Teresa was once asked why she did what she did, and she simply said 'for Jesus'. This centre always holds, it cannot be unhinged. It is a deeply personal relationship: we are led by Jesus 'one by one', known by name, not as one of a group. We follow him as one we know, not a stranger.

We study his life and times, getting to know the places and events of his life, we become familiar with the gospels and get to know him in the heart. Prayer is the way of keeping our centre of conviction and motivation strong. Freedom grows and we begin to find him everywhere.

Different types of people and spirituality stress different aspects of Jesus. The Eastern approach to Jesus is very much the 'way'; while the African is the 'life'. The European stress is the 'truth'. In Europe we need to rediscover also the joy and vibrancy of the African and Latin American expressions of faith, and also the presence of God in all life's moods and journeys of the Indian and Eastern traditions.

We can get so caught up in small or even big truths and doctrines that we miss other centres of faith. All faith needs the balanced approach to Jesus – way, truth and life.

Recall people who guided you well in your life. Pray for them.
Jesus, our way, guide me in life; Jesus, our truth,
teach me your meaning of life; Jesus, our life, love me always.

JOHN 14:15–21

6ᵀᴴ SUNDAY OF EASTER

No body now but yours

St Teresa's prayer is popular in this adaptation –

Christ has no body now but yours, no hands, no feet on earth but yours.

Yours are the eyes through which he looks with compassion on this world.

Yours are the feet with which he walks to do well.

Yours are the hands with which he blesses all the world.

Yours are the hands, yours are the feet,

You are his eyes, you are his body.

Christ has no body now but yours,

No hands, no feet on earth but yours.

Yours are the eyes through which he looks with compassion on this world.

Christ has no body now on earth but yours.

Jesus speaks in the gospel about being still alive, even after his death. Mostly we find Jesus alive in the love of others. The energy of love that is connected to the energy of God, for God is love. Other times we find God close to us in prayer; but where we can sense him alive mostly is in the ordinary and extraordinary loves of every day, in marriage, family, friendship and care for others.

Many of us do not realise that in this way we have been Christ-bearers. In listening to another, in care of all sorts, in putting ourselves out for the other, in working for justice and for peace the Spirit of God is alive and people are touched by God's love through the co-operation of ordinary men and women.

Pray a litany to some favourite saints.
Lord, make our love cheerful and kind.
Let us know always that human love reflects your love.

7TH SUNDAY OF EASTER: FEAST OF THE ASCENSION

Fully alive

I asked a woman once if Johnny was in the house. She pointed at a chair and said, 'if he was here he would be there.' He never moved far! Jesus – he is here and there. The risen lord has moved on, but he has not fully left us. His Spirit dwells in us.

The one who came to earth has now gone back to heaven, bringing with him all that is human. His body – the man of heaven and the God of earth – is now the church, and that's us.

Before we are of any denomination or group, we are Christ's. We are baptised into the church of Christ; we live out our faith in different denominations. Today is the feast of the whole church – we begin in him and end in him, like the Alpha and Omega, the beginning and the end, on the paschal candle. Our faith is also renewed through living with Jesus – we are partners in our mission. Our faith is also renewed in reading and praying the gospel each day.

On earth we are his body, with all our strengths and weaknesses, goodness and sin. Icons have Jesus smiling as he reaches heaven, smiling on us and living through us. We prepare for the way he is with us now next Sunday – in the Spirit. Where the qualities of the Spirit are alive, he is alive and well among us.

A breathing prayer – as you breathe in notice you are
breathing in the gift of life from God.
Holy Spirit, living in the church, living in Mary,
draw me more fully into your life.

JOHN 20:19–23

PENTECOST SUNDAY

Spirit alive

Someone dies and we say he kept his spirit alive to the end; or we say that 'his spirit lives on'. A word we talk of easily. It's something elusive, you can't pin it down. It comes from somewhere. Maybe from parents, a spirit of endurance or being able to make it through tough time; or from our prayer and faith. We talk of good team spirit, or of a person who kept joyful and courageous to the end. Today is the feast of the Spirit of God, alive, active and joyful.

The flame of the Spirit of love is the flame of God. The tongues of fire over the apostles and the followers of Jesus were flames of love, the Spirit of God that would burn on the inside forever.

Pentecost is the flame of God's own love, given to his followers to mark the birth of the community, the body of Jesus, the church.

It is the spirit of forgiveness always, a gift of the first Pentecost. Did this blow in our own country during the visit of the British queen, when the Good Friday Agreement and other peace agreements were signed, when the call came for a new reconciliation among people hurt badly in the times of the troubles?

Compassion, mercy, forgiveness and a hope for justice for all are gifts we ask from the Spirit who blows among us strongly today.

On each inbreath, pray 'Come, Holy Spirit'.
Holy Spirit, live in me and in all of us
as you lived in Mary and the apostles.

TRINITY SUNDAY

In the name

They looked down from heaven – the Father, Son and Holy Spirit – with love for their people. They could see men and women of all races, colours, ages, faiths, holiness and sin. They knew help was needed for the human race and waited a long time before the time was right.

The word of God, son of God, born before all ages, became one of us. We know the rest of the story. One of the persons of the Trinity became one of us, so that we could become like them. Jesus, Son of the eternal Father, was born, lived and died like us. In death, cruelly murdered and then laid in the tomb, the Spirit became alive in him, and now the Spirit of Jesus and the Father is alive in each of us since baptism.

The life of the Trinity becomes very ordinary in the love, care and forgiveness we offer to each other. It's also there in the ways in which we try to better the lives of the poor, the depressed and the anxious. It's in how we try to teach a younger generation the best lessons of humanity and faith, and introduce them to this mystery of God. We are active partners in the work of God, Father, Son and Holy Spirit in the world today.

Slowly make the sign of the cross a few times today,
asking to believe in the mystery of God's love within God and for us.
By the mystery of water and wine in the Mass, help us, Lord,
to share in the divinity of Christ,
who humbled himself to share in our humanity.

BODY AND BLOOD OF CHRIST / CORPUS CHRISTI

Real presence

The feast today highlights the central place of the Eucharist in Christian life, our faith that God becomes present in a real way in ordinary bread and wine – food for the journey of life in the bread, energy and joy for the journey of life in the wine. Bread and wine were very much part of the ordinary food of the people of his time, and also of their religious life. People would remember the bread in the desert and the wine of the coming of the Lord.

Each time we come to Mass, we take part in a real way in the death and resurrection of the Lord. The sacrifice of Christ on the cross and his resurrection is 'made present' among us. It is a place and time of grace.

So our Eucharist today is not just to commemorate something that happened many years ago. It is our commitment to Christ in his people, and our faith in his real presence among us in the Eucharist and in each other.

Jesus asks us to share the bread and cup, to proclaim this 'mystery of faith' for all time. We proclaim today that the Jesus of the tabernacle is the Jesus within all of us. Let's be amazed that in each of us, God dwells in Jesus Christ!

> *Recall moments when receiving communion*
> *gave you strength in your life.*
> *Lord, I believe in your presence in the Eucharist.*
> *Strengthen my belief.*

2ND SUNDAY IN ORDINARY TIME

Spiritual beings on a human journey

John the Baptist had been told to watch out for the Spirit of God. Somehow now he recognised the Spirit in Jesus. Somehow he knows that this new person, Jesus, will give this Spirit to all. We call it the Holy Spirit, the Spirit of Jesus.

We talk of team spirit, the spirit of generosity in a family, a bad spirit around. We have a spiritual life. We are more than we seem, more than a body. We are made for an eternal relationship with God, which begins now.

On Migrant Sunday, we think of the situations of asylum seekers and refugees. Many different sorts of migrants have come to our country. These are people who often treated badly in Ireland, in a system that seems not to be changing. They are people who for reasons of great danger cannot go back to their own country. They show us the Spirit of courage in the decision a parent has to make to bring their family to another land for a better life, or the Spirit of sacrifice that people make in detention centres and refugee camps.

We pay tribute also to volunteers and statutory workers who do their best for our refugees.

The Spirit is freely given to all of us. John recognised that in Jesus, and at Pentecost the new community of followers welcomed the outpouring of the Spirit. With God's help we can do the same: we can recognise the Spirit in us all, on our human journey of life.

Think of footage of refugees on TV;
ask for generosity of spirit to welcome them.
Holy Spirit, influence for goodness all I do and say.

3ᴿᴰ SUNDAY IN ORDINARY TIME

Love and call

We notice a big change of life for the disciples – they leave the past to follow the Lord, leaving behind their old jobs and roles, but also what might block them from living fully. To follow the Lord joyfully we need to believe in ourselves as valued in the sight of God. We pick up messages about ourselves from significant people and we may have to let them go. A child whose parents separate often feels unloved and needs the care and love that shows they are okay. Many addicted people have, deep down, a sense of not being loved. Every child coming into the world deserves to know that he or she is loved. We believe that the first gift of our faith is the love of God, the humble God who became one of us in love. In religion we need to touch into the love and the call of God, by gradually letting go of the things in this world that prevent us from knowing God's love. The first apostles had something new. Each of us, week by week, can get this new thing, the love of God. Everything else flows from that. To know the love of God is a huge gift, and to know the love and acceptance of another or a few others in life is also a huge gift. Both are one, in every love and friendship we have.

Is there anything keeping you from living in God's love?
Ask his help in this.
Lord, let me know your love day by day and share it with all I meet.

4ᵀᴴ SUNDAY IN ORDINARY TIME

Day-to-day compassion

Today's gospel is described by Pope Francis: 'This is the new law, the one we call "the Beatitudes". It's the Lord's new law for us' (February 2016). It highlights attitudes of the heart rather just than a set of rules to be followed.

We do not stay just with the words of Jesus. His life and teaching was a commentary on this sermon. Jesus invites us to watch how the sermon is lived in his life. All the qualities – being poor in spirit, able to mourn our losses and work for peace – are qualities of the humble person. This is when we know our need for God, our need for each other. Even in his risen life he was the humble one who could listen to the doubts of his disciples and guide them to further faith, each in his or her own way.

The church is called to live these qualities, which lead us to the compassion of Jesus and to being compassionate in our lives. Compassion and understanding come from listening deeply to others, especially to their joys and sorrows.

Compassion also grows in prayer – by asking for it, and by watching the compassion of Jesus in his life.

Someone working with young people once said that 'an ounce of listening is worth a ton of exhortation'. Marriage, friendship and family life are all enriched by the quality of compassionate listening.

*Some time today notice how you are feeling; share that with
Jesus in prayer. Notice too how these feelings affect
how you are with others during the day.
Thank you, Lord, for your compassion for me
in all the times of my life.*

5TH SUNDAY IN ORDINARY TIME

Salt for the Eucharist

In Galilee around the time of Jesus, there was a flourishing fishing industry. Peter, James and John were part of it, and they were big-time fishermen. Fish from Galilee went all over the then known empire, and to Rome along the trade route, which went through Galilee. It was kept fresh, as much food was, as we kept food fresh for years before freezers – by salting it. The word of God is kept fresh within us by prayer; otherwise our Christian life may become weak and tasteless.

A big food of Jesus is the Eucharist. His bread of life can go stale unless we 'salt' it. We salt the Eucharist by our lives. We keep the Mass alive by the way we live.

The Eucharist is entrusted to us. God gives us his Son, his food, and leaves it to us how we live by it.

Jesus invites us to be the 'salt of the earth' – to be people whose lives are centred on helping others and making the places around us places of kindness, compassion, hope, fun and life. We don't say, 'You're salt of the earth', if someone just receives communion. We are the salt of the earth if we live out our communion. The bread of Jesus is salted with the goodness of men and women, young and old, everywhere.

Our response then links in with the first reading – if we feed, shelter, clothe and help our neighbour, we are 'the light that rises in the darkness'.

Recall when you helped someone recently.
Give thanks you could do this.
Lord may your kingdom come in every part of the world.

6TH SUNDAY IN ORDINARY TIME

The heart of religion

This list of some of Jesus' sayings give an indication of what is important to him. He states the religious tradition of the people when he says that he has not come to abolish the old religion, and that religion must go much deeper and be an affair of the heart. He asks for forgiveness and reconciliation when he speaks about leaving a gift at the altar to go for reconciliation. He commends marriage, and faithfulness in marriage, in his views on divorce. He believes in the respect for sexuality that is shown in not using a person. This collection of Jesus' sayings form a background to how he lived his life himself. He lived out these sayings in many of the events of his life, which we hear about on other Sundays. The Sermon on the Mount, of which this is part, is the backdrop to much of Jesus' life and mission, a sort of vision statement for his life and ministry.

Much of this went against the religious practice of his people, which was centred mostly on externals. He saw the ritual and the law of religion as important only if it came from the heart.

This is the challenge always to religion – to live heartily what it enthusiastically believes. Practices in ritual and in religious custom and laws may change with different cultures and times; what is important is the way we live our lives, following Jesus and knowing that all our efforts to live like him are praised and rewarded. Pope Francis says, 'It is not enough to just respect the commandments and do nothing more. Christian life is not just an ethical life: it is an encounter with Jesus Christ' (9 May 2016).

Repeat a favourite gospel phrase as you breathe in;
your outbreath is your thanks for this help in your life.
Lord, your will be done each day in my life.

7TH SUNDAY IN ORDINARY TIME

Give to an enemy

This is quite a tough gospel. We sometimes like to get our own back. We know the desire for vengeance in family and other groups, and in national groupings. The 'eye for an eye' brings no peace, just a quiet lull in violence.

We know the opposite. People see the enemy walking the street and know that the only way forward is to make peace. This may not mean forgiveness immediately. Some can find a way forward only gradually.

The forgiveness of the gospel is a slow journey. We have small hurts and have ways of dealing with them. But the big ones are there too – maybe someone getting a job over someone dishonestly, being abused, family being mocked, bullying. Healing, freedom and forgiveness takes time.

We need to understand our own vengeance and at times forgive ourselves for it. The love of God is the love that helps us love the self in the normal hurts and grievances of life. The love of God is a grace, filling that space in us that is open to love – the grace of loving self and others.

To be perfect is to become like God in compassion and in love. This is a wonderful vision for ourselves, our church and our world. It is the dream of God that all God's children live in love, peace and justice.

Prayer helps ... can you bring someone to God – to the cross?
Pray with someone at the cross; it makes a difference.
Lord, help me to forgive and, when I cannot,
to be patient with myself as you are with me.

8TH SUNDAY IN ORDINARY TIME

God cares for what God creates

The gospel tells the story of lilies of the field and birds of the air after we are told that we can't serve God and money. God reminds us that he cares for us through weak things like flowers and birds, not money.

He praises poverty of mind and heart. A famous spiritual writer said while on retreat, 'I had a terrible sense of being inadequate. Not up to it. Full of weakness'. Another said, 'Don't be afraid you are inadequate, not up to it, full of weakness. Makes you know your need for care, and the call to care for each other'.

God's message always remembers the poor. Billions are starving and homeless today. Our prosperity and our wealth is for the glory of God too. We are to let money serve us. The main way we know that God cares is that people care for each other. We find that in all sorts of ways. This is always the big message of the gospel. It is not enough to pray, to meditate, just for its own sake. All is for the service of love in big and small ways.

Just remember you are worth more than anything around you, you are the image of God – and so is everyone else!

Picture someone very poor, weak, in trouble.
With that picture in mind, repeat the words 'God cares for us all'.
Lord, after I have rested in your presence,
send me out in your loving service.

9ᵀᴴ SUNDAY IN ORDINARY TIME

Deeds not words

A famous simple saying for St Ignatius Loyola is that 'love is proved in deeds, not words'. While words of compassion, gratitude and love are important, they are empty if not matched by the way we live. It is easy to pray, 'Lord, Lord', but more difficult to do the will of God.

God's will is that we love one another, that we try to make peace as we pray at Mass for 'peace, according to your will'. No matter what a person's faith or lack of faith, when they are trying to make peace, they are doing God's will. God's will is for a just world, and that we do our best in all we do for our immediate circle and for the common good.

Sometimes we need to discern, think, talk and grapple with what Jesus would do or say in any given situation. We are helped in this by prayer, but also by talking with one another in sincerity and honesty.

The 'Lord, Lord' of our prayers is to be matched with integrity in our lives.

Referring to the rock of our faith, Pope Francis names some whose lives are built on this rock of Jesus. Those who built on the rock of Jesus are the many saints:

> not necessarily canonised, but saints – men and women who put into practice the love of Jesus. And every day is the same, but they do not get bored because their foundation is the rock, Jesus. (December 2014)

Ask in prayer what the rock of your faith is – ask that it be more and more the love and call of Jesus.
Lord, thy will be done on earth as it is in heaven.

10TH SUNDAY IN ORDINARY TIME

The look of Jesus

Pope Francis says: 'Jesus' gaze always lifts us up. It is a look that always lifts us up … never lets us down … It invites us to get up … to move forward. The gaze makes you feel that He loves you. This gives the courage to follow Him' (September 2013). A famous painting of the calling of Matthew highlights Jesus' eyes meeting Matthew's across a room.

We find references in the scriptures to the look of God and the look of Jesus. At times people could return that look, at other times they hid from its glory and its love. Behind all the conversations of Jesus in the gospel, is his look. Even if they knew he could see into them, it was the look and the gaze of love. We know how we can look at someone we love and enjoy that look for hours. A parent gazing at a child, even when the child, a teenager, would ask them not to look at them like that in public!

We might think of Jesus looking over our family album or our pictures on a tablet or laptop, and, as we do in the family, he looks with joy and love at pictures over the years. Jesus first looks with the eye of mercy. He encourages us to look on others with the mercy and love that is the look of God. The call follows from his look.

Imagine Jesus with you; imagine that he looks at you with care and love. Enjoy that look, and be grateful.
Lord, may your look and your gaze bring me always to trust in you.

11TH SUNDAY IN ORDINARY TIME

Shepherds of the future

The gospel today presents the care of Jesus when he sees people in need. He knows he cannot help them alone. He asks us to pray for people who will work with him, and then calls others to do his work.

It's like a mother or father who is close to death ensuring that the children are cared for. Often a parent's thoughts are with the one who needs care most, worrying about what will happen 'when we are gone' to the child with special needs. Real love looks beyond the present to care into the future for those we love. Isn't that why we have the custom of godparents, who promise to look after the child, and, in the days when many parents died, would promise to bring them up?

Jesus needs each of us. Each of us can be his message of care and love for those around us, and for the wider world in its starvation, depression and special needs.

Each was called by name. This is a personal call to bring our particular qualities to Jesus. He is asking each of us to be the best person each of us can be, not a carbon copy of anyone else or any saint.

This call grows within the community of the church. Pope Francis remarks: 'No vocation is born of itself or lives for itself. A vocation flows from the heart of God and blossoms in the good soil of faithful people' (2014).

Maybe you met someone this week and knew they were in great need.
Ask God's help to respond as best you can.
Lord, teach me to be generous in your service.

12ᵀᴴ SUNDAY IN ORDINARY TIME

Just trust!

Our lives are lightened by people we can trust. We need to trust so much in life. We know the great pain when our trust is shaken by people we thought we could trust – parents, teachers, religious superiors, the church, friends and more. In the gospel today Jesus addresses that need and grace in our lives. He encourages us to place our trust in those who care for us, and to trust in God who does not want destruction, but development, who wants peace among people in all sorts of ways. In what do we trust? Pagola writes: 'some feel a need to consume more in order to feel secure; and seek a life of entertainment to forget their everyday problems' (The Gospel According to Matthew, p. 106). Jesus tells us to trust in God, who would not harm even a hair of our head. He asks and urges us to be people who would not harm another. We are worth this care and love just by being created. Like a parent or grandparent, or an aunt or uncle, totally loving a new child before the child is even seen, so God loves each of us. The sight of a starving child brings out our love and a desire to care.

This is linked to the care of God: in this care and trust of each other, we find the trust and care of God, given and received, for 'where there is love, there is God (1 John 3:7).

> *Just echo the word 'trust' as you sit in silence;*
> *let this gift and call of trust fill your being.*
> *Sacred heart of Jesus, I place all my trust in you.*

13TH SUNDAY IN ORDINARY TIME

The simple cup of water

The examples are stark in the gospel today: about not preferring mother and father to Jesus; about how, in our care for others, we care for Jesus, and how, in our neglect of others, we neglect him. We need to go beyond the practical example to finding out what is central in our lives and how we see God as central. When God is central, our love can be in the smallest of services to people, like 'the cup of cold water'.

Jesus is not central outside our humanity, and our human relationships. In the real needs of ordinary people we meet his needs. We give the 'cup of cold water' to the person who needs it, not just to Jesus. It's like many stories in the gospel of Jesus helping those in real need. This is the central point of faith.

We help in simple ways. This is what Pope Francis refers to in his encouragement of simple love, 'like the warm supper we look forward to at night, the early lunch awaiting someone who gets up early to go to work. Homely gestures. Like a blessing before we go to bed, or a hug after we return from a hard day's work. Love is shown by little things, by attention to small daily signs which make us feel at home. Faith grows when it is lived and shaped by love' (September 2015).

> *Recall a time when someone helped you in a small way.*
> *Be grateful. Offer yourself to do the same when you can.*
> *Make me, O Lord, a channel of your peace and love*
> *when I see the needs of others.*

14TH SUNDAY IN ORDINARY TIME

A time for rest

The invitation of Jesus to find peace in his presence is one of the most popular of his sayings. He is contrasting his message with the burdensome law, which somehow had lost the heart of religion, over-emphasising the externals of laws and rituals. He is not devaluing laws and rituals but putting them in their place. He offers an invitation that everyone can hear; and at many times of life we really need to hear it. These may be times of illness, bereavement, anxiety, depression and worry. It is an invitation to come into his presence, which is a loving presence. It's not just an invitation to enjoy a restful time, but to rest in the presence of love.

Any notion we have of Jesus that is harsh is false: he is 'gentle and humble in heart'. This is the atmosphere he asks us all to spread. 'Once you have received the refreshment and comfort of Christ, we are called in turn to become refreshment and comfort for our brothers and sisters, with a meek and humble attitude, in imitation of the Master' (Pope Francis, July 2014).

The church is a place of rest for the weary; the place where we find encouragement in the ordinary situations in our lives, where we are called to respond to those who suffer through poverty, homelessness and many other unjust social situations that are part of our world, near and far.

Recall last week where you needed to hear these words,
or met someone else who needed to hear them, maybe through you.
Speak to the Lord in your own words.
Take into your hands, Lord, the burdens in my life;
help me to trust in you.

15TH SUNDAY IN ORDINARY TIME

Love is never lost

The gospel is a story about people trying to do well and often not much comes from it. One mother said, 'I hope I'll see some of my children at the altar again before I die'. A football trainer said, 'I wish we won matches when he was in school – but the fruit of all the hours came later when he scored goals for the county!'

A big point of this story is about the fruits – 30-, 60-, 100-fold. When we work at love or faith, the deeper things of life, something good happens.

We try to hand on faith in the family and school situations. Sometimes we feel we see little return for our work. Or we give time to the family in many ways and see little return for our love.

The consoling point of the story – we never know when or where there will be the fruits of our love ... Love given is never lost. Like dropping something into the river, you never know where it will end up. Love given to children in the family may bear fruit in the next generation. We never know. Good may be done in a son's or daughter's new country from the seeds of faith planted at home.

Part of life is trial and effort. Jesus' attitude was the same. He 'threw' out love like the sower throws out the seed. He knows it may fall on hard ground, but he gives it anyway. He gave love on Calvary to everyone. God is like that. It may take years to flower. God doesn't stint the seed, nor does he stint love.

On your inbreath, echo the word 'love'.
On the outbreath send this love to someone who may need it now.
May I live, Lord, in your love that never ends?

13: 24–43

16ᵀᴴ SUNDAY IN ORDINARY TIME

Small beginnings

Everything starts small. The mustard seed was a tiny seed that grew into a flowering bush; it was not mustard as we know it, but only a bush to give beauty and shelter. It can remind us of the beauty of creation, and of the caring shelter we can give to others. It is also a reminder that each of us began as a seed in the mother's body, and grew with the plan of God. The love of God grows like that – it begins small with birth and with baptism, and then grows wide so that we share our love of God. It is the same with marriage – love begins and then grows so that children and grandchildren and others may shelter in love. Love grows when love is given, in our immediate circle, and in our care for the wider world. Good friendship and love spreads out to many.

We want the kingdom of God on earth and God is saying that it grows slowly. It grows as we try to grow love, peace, justice and compassion. The shelter of the mustard bush is the mercy of God, encouraging our parish to be 'an oasis of mercy' (Pope Francis). It is not easy, as love and care for the really needy often meets with opposition. The kingdom of God grows with the help of God, and without this help, our efforts are in vain.

Recall something in your life that began small
and has now grown; give thanks.
Lord, may your kingdom come among us.

17TH SUNDAY IN ORDINARY TIME

The good, the bad, and the treasure

Jesus takes the ordinary for his story, asking what you would really want never to lose, asking what your treasure is. Is it money, reputation, locality? 'I gave up a better job but had time for the family and for love'; words of a young father. We know that parents give up a lot for their children; as do grandparents, godparents and others. As people we look for what's most important in life: the love of God; deep and enduring friendships, success after hard work in school, commitment to the poor – what cannot be lost and what is worth sacrificing other good things for.

Life is a mixture of the good and the bad. There is an old Dublin saying: 'There's good in the worst of us and bad in the best of us.' We work for God with the strengths and weaknesses of all we work with. God sows the seed of the gospel in good and bad soil; it bears fruit in its own way wherever it is sown. The treasure is in our people. So much hidden generosity comes out at bad times – floods, power cuts, illness and death. We need always to find the hidden treasures in our own people and even in our history. The kingdom of God is close, near and is within us.

Think of what you really value in life. Take time.
Give thanks to God for what brings deep joy in life.
Thy Kingdom Come, Lord Jesus.

18TH SUNDAY IN ORDINARY TIME

Feeding the needy

Pope Francis remarks:

> We find Jesus' wounds in carrying out works of mercy, caring for the body of your wounded brother, because he is hungry, because he is thirsty, because he is naked, because he is humiliated, because he is a slave, because he is in jail, because he is in the hospital. Those are the wounds of Jesus today. And Jesus asks us to take a leap of faith, towards him, but through his wounds in his people today. We need to touch the wounds of Jesus, we must caress the wounds of Jesus, we need to bind the wounds of Jesus with tenderness, and we have to kiss the wounds of Jesus, and this literally. Just think of what happened to St Francis, when he embraced the leper. (May 2016)

This is what is behind Jesus' wish to feed the hungry. He feeds bread for physical hunger, but the story of the gospel today is more than bread for hungry people. It is getting fully involved in the lives of those in need. It is the calling of the church: to practise the works of mercy.

Any Christian group, parish or otherwise, tries to reach out to those most in need in their area. Today the hungry need to be fed, refugees and homeless need a home, and those wounded by life need healing. The call of the church is truly to be 'the field hospital' of Jesus and his disciples in the world.

Think of someone really poor; see Jesus beside him or her.
Pray as you feel drawn.
Give us today, O Lord, and to all our world, our daily bread.

19TH SUNDAY IN ORDINARY TIME

A hand to be held

A most strange gospel story – Jesus walks on the water. It's the type of gospel that suits a decision time, challenging us into deep trust – an invitation to come to the water; not to be afraid. It's about trusting in Jesus, when there is nothing else. If you have human help, it's great – but not the same as trusting in God.

In time of death, the call is to trust in God's promise, because he is the way and the truth. Old age can be the same, or times in life when we just don't know what the future will hold. It sounds unusual, but what Jesus does in this situation is very human. He doesn't lecture or say a prayer, he just holds hands. Someone was given a book on bereavement after a family death – he said he needed a hand to be held, or his tears to be heard. That's Jesus. He held Peter. God is a God with skin, with a human heart, and leaves big ideas behind when we are in trouble. Jesus just went across the lake, stopping his comfortable prayer.

There are times when we just need to hold on to God in trust. On another occasion Peter would jump into the lake again – after the resurrection. Always a water man! Then he would be asked not just to hold a hand, but to be the hand that would reach out to others. Peter was prepared for his mission in many ways. As Pope Francis says, 'When the Lord wants to give us a mission, wants to give us a task, He prepares us. He prepares us to do it well' (June 2014).

Remember a time when all you seemed to have was God; thank him.
Or recall when all you needed was God; ask him now for help.
Lord, in you I put my trust.

20TH SUNDAY IN ORDINARY TIME

Fighting for her child

She was a woman like many. She would fight for her child, so she took on Jesus, the best known religious figure around. Like someone taking on the minister for health or children over a medical card for a chronically ill child, and not letting them off the hook. Jesus was testing her. He saw faith, but he wanted everyone else to see it. So he told her she didn't fit into the local religious sphere because she was foreigner, like an asylum seeker or a refugee. She knew she fitted into the heart of Jesus simply because she was the mother of a sick child and believed he could help.

Even if he would cure everyone, maybe he would come back to her at the end. Jesus went further – he cured her child and praised her faith.

She is another of the unnamed ones of the gospel. Like the woman of Samaria, the rich young man, the thief on Calvary – she is herself, and she is all of us. She is everyone, man and woman, of faith.

Faith in a surprising God who, in Jesus, his Son, never says no to goodness. Faith that keeps us energetic and alive, not tired, in soul as well as body.

Remember your feeling of gratitude for the children of your family.
Lord, I believe, strengthen my faith.

21ST SUNDAY IN ORDINARY TIME

Nothing but Jesus

We all need some statements like Peter's that give a rock and a meaning to life. It gives us a clue of where we belong at deeper levels. We all need statements that express our faith in God. For Peter it was his faith in Jesus, the son of God. This would keep him going all of his life, even at times of unfaithfulness and danger. He could never forget that he had said, 'you are the Christ, the son of the living God'.

We might wonder who or what is a living God for us? Where we might put our basic trust? What is it that, if taken away, we would be lost without? We can give our lives to family, country, a political party, money. Some of these are worth our trust and some not so much.

We need the rock that Peter found in Jesus. He was called rock only because of his relationship with Jesus Christ, the one who calls forth our faith and love and gives our lives a huge meaning.

It's not that we have nothing but Jesus – it's that we can integrate all that is important in life within our trust in him. It is God who reveals Jesus to us.

We want to give this to our younger people – a rock they can stand on in life, which nothing can demolish. This is Jesus, and in him all is created.

Recall strong convictions in your life.
Ask that they may be strengthened.
Lord, be my rock, my stronghold, my safety.

22ND SUNDAY OF THE YEAR

The third day

We meet deep human concerns and feelings in the gospel today. Peter is shocked to the core that Jesus would die; so shocked that he always later seemed to forget that Jesus promised that he would rise on the third day. Jesus talks very seriously about the cost of following him, like the cost of following any commitment in life.

Jesus invites us to live at the deepest level of ourselves. In the area of life where we live and love, laugh and cry, worry and enjoy, hurt and forgive. In all these very personal sides of life, Jesus dwells, since he says that he makes his home in us.

We can call it a sort of 'third day' hope. Nothing except love, which is eternal, was final for Jesus. For all the worst things of life there was a third day. The day on which hope would be fuller than any despair, and when life would be more lasting than death. Jesus was like that – when people met him, they remembered him and remembered how he touched the fears and anxieties of their lives with a deep hope.

We are 'third day' people, knowing that the love and life of God, promised at our baptism, will always be in the air around us, filling us with the breath of God, and breathing fragrance all around us like the best of flowers. Later they would be raised from final despair and hopelessness at his resurrection. But it took time!

Breathing in and out, receive the peace of God.
On the inbreath, let the word 'peace' echo within you.
Lord, may I never lose faith in you.

23RD SUNDAY OF THE YEAR

Each other's keepers

In any group, small and big, things cause friction. Everyone thinks his or her way is right. We can fight over who is right. Some things are worth a fight, others not.

In the big questions of life, we need the advice, support and love of the other. Many people ask themselves, 'Why I didn't give an honest opinion about a decision like marriage or a job or a course of studies which seemed ill-advised to everyone?' We all have good and not-so-good tendencies. We can only advise as best we can, sensitively and wisely, and hope we get a hearing.

We are afraid to hurt, to be rejected. Why do we let so many people drink themselves into trouble and never tell them? The terror of a neighbourhood, no matter what age, needs to be confronted. The problem of drugs in a neighbourhood is not confronted. Crime is not reported.

In small and big things we are each others' keepers. Jesus is saying something like that today. Parents can find this difficult as they try to guide the family well and not lose them. We have social responsibility in the family and in the neighbourhood and even worldwide for the common good.

God wants the best for each of us. We can help each other to goodness, we can support each other, advise each other, pray for and with each other, and help each other on our way to God.

Recall an occasion when another gave good advice,
even when you may not have liked it at the beginning. Be grateful!
Give me wisdom, Lord, when others ask me for advice or an opinion.

24TH SUNDAY IN ORDINARY TIME

Forgiveness

We are called to forgive; and that can be really difficult. You have been defrauded by the banks of your life's savings – can you forgive? You were abused as a child – can you forgive? You were done out of a job because another lied to get it – can you forgive? The answer is maybe 'no'. What then does God want? He asks us to open our hearts to the other so that we may forgive. Forgiveness is the deepest of God's desires on our behalf, and he hopes that we can forgive each other.

Our hurts and burdens are heavy to carry through life. To forgive can release some of that weight. The person who hurt us may be dead, or may not even know (or care) that we are hurting. When we desire to forgive but don't know how, one way of looking for this strength is to pray for it. We often pray, *'Lord, make my heart like yours'*. When we pray that we are praying to be forgiving people!

Another way is to pray for the person. When we realise that as God loves me, he also loves everyone, we may find a spark or light of forgiveness in our souls.

Out of this we may find the will to meet the other and talk to him or her, and find the grace of forgiveness between us.

Forgiveness sometimes comes slowly. When God sees us wanting to be on the road to forgiveness, he gives us the graces we need to unburden ourselves and be able to love like him.

*Sit in silence for a while, and send a blessing or prayer
to someone you need to forgive.
Lord, I ask – make my heart like yours.*

25ᵀᴴ SUNDAY IN ORDINARY TIME

Deserving our rights

We often say that people don't deserve welfare or food if they don't work. We can be stingy in judging what others deserve and need.

Jesus has a new way. We deserve our rights even when we do the least. The denarius was a day's wage, enough to live on. There are certain rights we all have – to have food and a job are two of them. These people wanted to work. We are rewarded by God for who we are, not for what we do.

Jesus' vision is that everyone deserves to earn enough to live on.

> To believe in a God who is an unconditional Friend, is to have the most liberating experience that one could imagine. On the contrary, to live in the presence of an avenging and threatening God could change us into the most dangerous and self-destructive neurotics. We need to learn not to confuse God with our own narrow and stingy plans. We sometimes wish to distort God's un-fathomable goodness. (José Pagola).

That's the way the kingdom of God grows. It grows within us in thanks and sharing. That's what we do at every Mass. Success for Jesus is not the amount we do, but that we do things with a full heart.

Recall the picture of a dole queue or a provision centre and pray.
Lord, may all I do this day and week begin with your inspiration
and end with your pleasure. Amen.

26TH SUNDAY IN ORDINARY TIME

Grumpy brother and honest brother

Two brothers: the second was grumpy, honest and generous; the first was kindly, confused and selfish. We know often people who do what they say, who do something in the end, or who don't do what they say. The first man knew his mind and then did what was right. Is it the message of this humorous and honest story that sincerity and integrity are important? A certain spirituality ignores ourselves – it's all about doing. Grit your teeth and get down to it. Roll up your sleeves and work ... but 'nobody asked us how we were'. But we find God both in the discernment and in the doing. In the end we must know how we feel about something and then put that in the hands of God and in prayer and do what seems right. The Lord wants the follow through! We need to take time to decide well – the first son did not do that. Then we need to follow and do what is right.

We need sound heads, compassionate hearts and willing hands. The vineyard is where we live all the time. The call is to live in truth, love and justice. We need to believe in the possibilities of a better world, and to become people who can decide on what is right in the sight of God and do it. We will often resist. We want to do what is right and do the opposite. He understands our mixed motivation. In all of that we need the Christian vision and a desire to do the world a world of good.

Recall a time you felt resentful about doing what you ought to do.
How did you feel after doing it?
Lord, may everything I do begin with you
and be happily ended in love. Amen.

27TH SUNDAY IN ORDINARY TIME

The vineyard is ourselves!

God is all the time caring for his people and thinking of us, making sure we're not endangered when he can help it. His care for his people goes into the heart of the Trinity, one of whom becomes one of us, for our sake.

He wants us to bear fruit, as in the second reading. He will give these fruits – and wants us to value them.

In our society today, we could say that in many countries child protection and care is better, We are more inclusive of people who differ from us and the church is open to the whole human family. In Ireland we have more peace now than we had, but maybe not more justice, especially for our migrant people. These are some fruits. We miss out on some issues – the value of faith and community is low and sometimes in public or political life we go for the temporary and the illusory and the dramatic. The gap between rich and poor is wider than ever. We have had bad experiences of greed and financial abuse, even in the charities sector. Our care of the elderly leaves much to be demanded.

Looking at the gospel vision, we can ask how the vineyard is nourished. We find that the cornerstone of the Christian way of life is love, and the love is a person in Jesus. He is the one who will invigorate the vine ... Some will ignore him, some will follow. All of us are probably a bit in between. God sent his own Son into the vineyard of human life, not because life is perfect, but because love is. Jesus comes among us because we need him.

Imagine a situation where people try to do well
and are prevented. Pray for them.
Lord, may your kingdom come, here and now, today.

28ᵀᴴ SUNDAY IN ORDINARY TIME

Look to the heart

There is a big problem with this story. In a good story Jesus always raises a question. It seems a bit unfair to be thrown out, having been brought in at the last minute, because you had no garment. However, the garment means you want to be there and to take on the values of the feast. The garment is the desire of the heart to be a follower in name and deed.

God invites all, but expects us to come with a good heart. Often we see people around mass who seem not to respect it. They may not come often, but God looks to the desires of the heart. Maybe the non-churchy parents who want their child baptised know deep down that their love for the child brings them to baptism. Is that not a good reason? Or maybe the young people who come to mass because they have exams coming up and need all the help they can get?

While Jesus is totally the inviting one, he wants us to remain with him. The heart that follows is the heart that wants to love, and that desire is the wedding garment.

The man knew in his heart that he should not be there. Jesus sees into the heart. What we look for is the sincerity in what brings us to God and that can be different for everybody. Religion is firstly of the heart, and then practice. We never know what's in the heart of our people who sometimes come in faith. You never can tell! Let God be the judge of that!

Recall a time you felt invited by God to help a neighbour.
Offer that thanks to God now.
Lord, make my heart compassionate like yours.

29TH SUNDAY IN ORDINARY TIME

A place for everything!

My mother used always say – put things where they belong. Newspapers, food, the bicycle not in the hall, and other homely advice. Jesus says the same here – give what belongs to where it belongs and to whom.   So Jesus is being asked about taxes and politics. He knows he is being trapped about money. He moves on to higher questions. Something about the answer of Jesus asks us – where do we belong?

Belonging can sound heavy – as if we are being controlled, or our money belongs to us and we can do what we like with it. But for Jesus it's the belonging of love, not of power and control.

Much is not in our control. We are born and die at God's time. This reminds us that we are not the masters of our lives, we come from God and go to God. This belonging is the centre of our human family and community. God doesn't want to control us but to love us.

But there's an addition: belonging to God means belonging to each other. We have rights and duties of love. To give to others what belongs to others; give to the poor what belongs to the poor. Everyone has a right to the food of the earth and the food of the mind, and shelter for the body. It's not charity when people are given food, education, a home, freedom of religion, freedom of speech – it is justice. To give to God what belongs to God is to share the goods of the earth!

Think of a time when you made a decision for the common good –
money given away, cleaning the neighbourhood,
joining a parents' group etc. Remember and be grateful.
Lord, may your will that we share well the goods of the world be done.

30TH SUNDAY IN ORDINARY TIME

The energy of true religion

'To love God and love your neighbour' – this is one of the most attractive of the sayings of Jesus. It is an encouragement to live fully with what brings the greatest joy in life – true love of God and the neighbour. It is at the heart of good religion, and what attracts many to Jesus.

Bad religion puts law above love. Bad religion fights for the partial truth of religion. We risk being victims of bad religion, just as we can be victims of bad nationalism, bad psychology or any other bad way of living. Jesus' life was to propose good religion and to live by it. The religion of some of the Pharisees was bad, in that it was incomplete in its scope.

We admire those who give energy in love and service. We are proud of people we know whose lives make a great and good difference to others. We know that our family and neighbourhood, parish and school, workplace and leisure time have been enriched by the self-sacrificing love of many people, young and old.

'He gave it his all' – we say that of a good player at the end of a match. We say of parents that they 'were always there for the children'. May we give all we have in our lives, giving in love, knowing that all we give is itself a gift from God, the giver of all good gifts.

Picture Jesus with a sick person; watch him touching the person.
This would be against the law! What would you say to him?
Lord, let love be the guiding principle of all I say and do and think.

31ST SUNDAY IN ORDINARY TIME

Love thy neighbour

We are often asking what the essence of our religion might be. Some people think of the different rules or what religion gives importance to. Jesus is quite clear when he is asked about the essence of religion: it is 'to love God and love your neighbour'. Anything else about our religion flows from this.

We hear it so often that we may get tired of it. When Jesus quoted it for the people he spoke to, they recited it a few times every day. It's like humming a favourite song; these are words to bring us life.

We wonder how we can grow in fulfilling this, or in appreciating it. Our memory is an important source of inspiration. Can you remember times when you loved your neighbour – people near and far, occasions when you know you were doing something out of love? We think of family examples with our children and the elderly where we gave time when they were in need. Times when we volunteered to improve the standard of life in our area, or gave time as a volunteer abroad. Memory is a way of finding energy from this command.

Another inspiration is the life of Jesus: he was one whose whole life was loving God his Father and the neighbour. Read the gospel of Mark and just watch how his love goes out to so many people, especially the ones like the leprosy patients and the foreigner that others would ignore.

This is the way of life of these commandments! The love and care of the neighbour is a sign of our love for God.

Repeat for a few minutes in prayer the mantra 'Love your neighbour
as yourself'. Lord, may your will be done on earth;
may we love our Father and our neighbour.

32ND SUNDAY IN ORDINARY TIME

Jesus – always new

The lamp is the light of love and of hope, and at the centre is the light of Christ. The light is given to us in many ways in our lives – it shines within as an internal joy, and outwards to many others. Jesus often advises, 'keep your lamps burning', and 'let your light shine'.

Like when the bulb goes out when the electricity fails, the lamp can go out without oil. The people of the gospel felt foolish that they had not brought oil with them to light their way. The oil is prayer and our relationship with Jesus. This is the essence of Christian life. Our Christian life is following a real, loving person; it is an invitation to get to know Jesus, and to find ourselves drawn from our hearts to follow him. Without this living relationship with Christ, words sound empty. We sometimes hear someone speaking of their Christian faith and cannot help wondering if it comes from the inside or is just a list of things to be believed and read.

Ignatius of Loyola's famous prayer is the prayer of the follower of Jesus: 'Lord, teach me to know you more, love you more, and serve you more faithfully in my life' (Spiritual Exercises). The 'more' indicates that this is never a finished product: like love and friendships it grows in our lives. It is exciting that Jesus is never gone from us; risen from the dead he is always alive, always new. Our reading of the gospel, our sharing at Mass and the sacraments and our personal prayer keep this relationship always alive, always new.

Thinking of a bright lamp, or imagining one,
ask for an ever-brightening light of Christ in your life.
Lord, teach me to know, love and serve you more faithfully every day.

33RD SUNDAY IN ORDINARY TIME

Well done!

Why did he hide the money? Maybe he was being asked to be dishonest – to use the money for purposes that diddled others. At the time of this parable most money was made dishonestly. Today this could be like trafficking in drugs or sex, treating our migrant workers badly, paying off violence or buying in a way that diminishes others. The servant was an honest man and suffered for it.

Did you feel you were compromised by being asked to do something you knew was wrong? A person pressurised into watching internet porn, or engaging in sexual activity, or trying out alcohol or drugs? They may feel they will suffer in the future if they don't give in.

The godfathers of crime and drugs and violence have a lot to answer for. They are those who make money at the expense of others. This is one way of reading this parable: that people try to get people to do their dirty work, and they can punish them for not doing it.

The man in the end got thrown out by the greedy master – but from God he will hear, 'Well done, come inherit the kingdom.'

Today we are encouraged by the man who would not do dirty work for anyone, would not take part in schemes that damaged others, and is the one who really 'did well'.

*Can you imagine a time when you or someone
you know went 'against the tide'.
Imagine Jesus saying to you, well done. What might it be for?
Lord, may I live faithful to you always.*

FEAST OF CHRIST THE KING

The 'I' word!

We know this story well. The most important word in it is 'I'. Jesus identifies himself with the people he is talking about. He doesn't just say people were in prison and you visited them, or sick, or naked. He says it is 'I' who am in prison, sick and naked. It's even more than being a brother or sister of Jesus. He identified totally with each of us, especially in need. Created as we are in the image of God, Jesus sees right through us to see God. God is the divine life in each person.

That makes the difference. We don't help the needy person only because he or she is needy, but because each is in the image of God and Jesus sees him or her and says, 'That's me'.

This can be a programme for life. For the young – can you make a decision about your life that includes deep care from your love of those in need? For those in their busy lives already and who have chosen their way – how can you show deep care and love for those in need? For the elderly – can you pray for those in need each day and encourage those more active to care for them?

Did you feed the hungry, give drink to the thirsty, welcome the stranger, clothe the naked, care for the sick and visit the prisoner?
Lord Jesus, may your kingdom come – the reign
of equality, justice, peace and love.

MISSION SUNDAY

Remembering our missionaries

This is a day to remember missionaries, and one I remember is Fr Frank. He was a Jesuit who worked in Zambia. Like many he left Ireland for three years in 1956 to work as a teacher before ordination and learn the language. After ordination he returned to parishes in Zambia until 1998. I remember him, and others, visiting our school, introducing us to the world of Africa, Japan and Hong Kong.

It was both an exciting life for them, and frustrating and lonely. Like many of their sisters in the women's congregations, they would come home only every six years, in the days when long-haul flights were expensive.

We salute them today, many of them in the nursing homes of their religious congregation who try to look after them well.

They did all this to follow Jesus; to bring the kingdom of God into education and parishes, and to bring health care to a new world. They wanted to make the world of the poorer nations better, and, in many ways, they succeeded. They are followed today by many who want to do the same, in ways suited to today.

Mission Sunday is a reminder to pray for our people helping in the struggle for faith and justice, equality and peace in many countries. They need our prayers and our help, and we are proud of them.

They want to want to carry out God's vision for the world: a world more equal, merciful and loving, and thus a holier place for people to live in.

Can you recall someone working as a missionary? Pray for them as they come to mind. May we in our parish, Lord, remember to support the church in other parts of the world?

DECEMBER 8:
FEAST OF THE IMMACULATE CONCEPTION OF OUR LADY

Beginnings

The gospel chosen for many feasts of Mary is the annunciation, the occasion when she was visited by an angel of heaven and asked to be the mother of God. It's as if this is the biggest moment of her life and it is recalled when we celebrate her memory.

Not only was it her big day, it is also the big day of the world. The world would never be the same because of Mary's 'yes' to the invitation to be the mother of God. Because of Mary, God is with us in a totally new way in the world, in the person of the human and divine Jesus.

Later in their lives, Jesus would praise Mary not just for being the physical mother, but because she 'heard the word of God and kept it'. She kept the word of God close to her heart, as she kept the body of Jesus close to herself in her womb and in her family life.

At the cross she would hear Jesus again, in one of his last words, call her 'mother', giving her to us as mother of the church. She still has a mothering role in the community of Jesus, the role of comfort and consolation. She nurtures us in prayer and through the scripture, so that we too become people who 'give birth' to Jesus in the world.

For her special role, the church has believed her to be free from any influence of sin from the first moment in the womb.

This was God's first gift to her. Her faith and motherhood is
her gift to us. Echo the word 'mother' as you breathe in and out.
Pray in whatever way you feel drawn.
Holy Mary, mother of God, pray for us now and always.

2:1–12

6 JANUARY:
FEAST OF THE EPIPHANY OF OUR LORD

Your star

The journey of the wise men is a story of the journey of life, of guidance on the way, of delight in finding faith and God, of the intrigue of a greedy and jealous king, and of the good overcoming the bad. We like the end of the story when the wise men outwit Herod, the good heroes win in a pantomime.

The star started them on the journey and then guided them to the end. The star that shone at our baptism is the promise of God to guide us through life. Faith grows through the ordinary events of life. What can seem ordinary happenings can be extraordinary grace – the birth of a child in your family, the first time you fall in love, the people you meet who make a big difference in life, success in a job, becoming a grandparent, an aunt, an uncle – anything creative in your life is a grace of God.

Your faith may have grown during a retreat when you learned how to pray in a deeper way, during a time you felt you really helped some people, or when you found yourself really listening and talking with someone, helping another or yourself to cope with problems.

Each of us has our own personal star guiding us – the star of prayer, love, friendship, support … the star has a different name at different times.

> *Be grateful for your star – and be grateful that you*
> *have been a star for others.*
> *Guide us, O God, and protect us kindly now,*
> *and at the hour of our death. Amen.*

17 MARCH: FEAST OF ST PATRICK

Youth and Faith

There are many legends about Patrick. Why did that story about snakes become associated with Patrick, since it is commonly believed that there were never snakes in Ireland? The reason is thought to be that in the Bible, snakes are often seen as a symbol of evil and the story of Patrick driving snakes out of Ireland demonstrates the power of Christianity to challenge and overcome evil. What might he throw out today? The evil of drugs, power/corruption, abuse of others of any sort, extreme greed. He would try to bring us to God so that whatever is evil would be overcome. His commitment was to spread the gospel of faith in Jesus Christ.

Patrick is an example of young faith, finding God in his late teens and then committing himself for good. He gives us a spur to believe in our young people, and that what we do for the faith of youth is always worth it.   From his experience of slavery in his youth, he became a mediator and a peacemaker. He is at the centre of all the churches in Ireland. Today Patrick would also look for the good in any culture, including that of the people who come to our shores.

He was a man Christ – of faith, of the gospel, of the church and of prayer. In his exile he was a man of tolerance. May his memory keep alive in us our love of gospel, church and prayer.

Call to mind people you love who are away from home
and pray for them.
Christ be near in all I do and say.

15 AUGUST:
FEAST OF THE ASSUMPTION OF MARY

As she is we now shall be

Today's feast is about the glory of death. We wonder much about what happens after death. What will we be like, will we recognise each other? Jesus says little about the details of the afterlife except that he goes to prepare us a place, and we will enjoy eternal life. The feast of Mary's Assumption throws some light on the mystery of death. We believe that she is body and soul in heaven. This means that she is totally there, knowing God and her son fully.

Our prayers have always linked Mary to our death. We pray 'now and at the hour of our death'. We will all need comfort at the time of our death. It can be a lonely time, often fearful and bewildering. Mary supports and loves us in prayer from heaven. In many places the Assumption is a harvest time feast. Death is for all of us the time of harvest when God welcomes us home with the fruit of our lives. Mary's harvest was rich. We hope ours will be similar; in many simple ways we help each other along the way. While Mary's feast puts our eyes on the final harvest, it also asks us to make sure of a harvest of goodness and kindness and faith each day.

Think of a picture of Mary you like or a place connected with Mary.
Say a prayer to her or a decade of the rosary.
Holy Mary, mother of God, pray for us, sinners,
now and at the hour of our death. Amen.

1 NOVEMBER: FEAST OF ALL SAINTS

Saints: a window on God

A child was once asked for a definition of a saint. She said 'a stained-glass window'! Asked why, she answered, 'The different colours let in the light and every saint is a different colour of God.' Every one of our unknown saints coloured God in a new way in his or her corner of the globe. On All Saints' Day we are grateful for the lives of so many people of every age, church and century who have done as best they could in following Jesus Christ.

Some of these people are canonised, each portraying strongly some aspect of Jesus. Today also recalls the millions of unknown saints in our families, neighbourhoods and communities who inspire us by their example.

Saints are not for our imitation. We can be holy only according to our own personality. But holy people inspire us to live our own Christian life. We know the limitations also of the anonymous holy people, and we are inspired by how our family and community 'saints' grew in the love of God within their ordinary human weaknesses.

The feast today is a grateful feast. The people we remember are like the tombs of the unknown soldier in many European cities, commemorating the soldiers who died and whose names may be forgotten. Maybe every church should have a shrine to the unknown saint, representing the people we remember today!

Who have been 'saints' for you? Recall what inspired you about them.
For your saints, O Lord, with you in glory we give thanks.

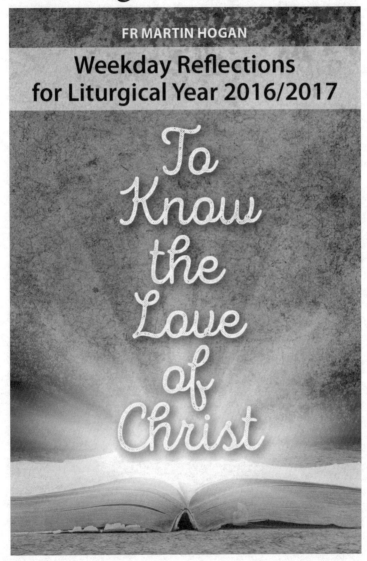

Also available from
Messenger Publications

www.messenger.ie   Phone: 353 1 7758522